Delicious Starbucks Beverage Recipes

Learn How to Make Your Favorite Starbucks Beverages with These Fast & Easy Starbucks Beverage Recipes

Jennifer James

© 2012   All rights reserved.

All Rights Reserved.   No part of this publication may be reproduced in any form or by any means, including scanning, photocopying, or otherwise without prior written permission of the copyright holder.

Disclaimer and Terms of Use: The Author and Publisher has strived to be as accurate and complete as possible in the creation of this book, notwithstanding the fact that he does not warrant or represent at any time that the contents within are accurate.

All recipes contained within were verified at that time. They have not been altered in this digital edition, and may refer to ingredients and cooking methods no longer available or practiced, respectively.

Readers are advised to always employ modern food safety practices, and avoid any actions that seem ill-advised. The author or publisher cannot be held responsible or liable for any consequences, losses, or damages that come about as a result of the use of this book.

While all attempts have been made to verify information provided in this publication, the Author and Publisher assumes no responsibility for errors, omissions, or contrary interpretation of the subject matter herein.

Any perceived slights of specific persons, peoples, or organizations are unintentional. Readers are cautioned to reply on their own judgment about their individual circumstances to act accordingly. This book is not intended for use as a source of legal, business, accounting or financial advice. All readers are advised to seek services of competent professionals in legal, business, accounting, and finance field.

Table of Contents

Caramelized Espresso Frappe
Caramel Apple Cider
Caramel Macchiato
Cappuccino-Chocolate Coffee Cake
Chai Tea
Chocolate Cappuccino Mousse
Coffee Banana Smoothie
Coffee Italian Ices
Double Chocolate Chip Crème
Frappuccino
Eggnog Latte
Frozen Cappuccino
Frozen Cappuccino #2
Frozzen Caramel Frappucino
Frozzen Frappucino
Frozzen Mocha Frappucino
Gingerbread Latte
Harvest Coffee Cider
Hot Mocha
Iced Constantine Coffee
Iced Espresso
Iced Caramel Macchiato
Irish cream espresso

[Java Float](#)
[Minty Hot Mocha](#)
[Mocha Java](#)
[Mocha Mudslide](#)
[Mocha Coconut Frappuccino](#)
[Mocha Slush](#)
[Peppermint Mocha](#)
[Pumpkin Spice Latte](#)
[Simple One Cup Chai](#)
[Starbucks Chai Tea](#)
[Starbucks Frappuccino](#)
[Starbucks Frozen Frappuccino](#)
[Starbucks Vanilla Iced Coffee](#)
[Starbucks White Chocolate Mocha](#)
[Starbucks Spiced Holiday Coffee](#)

[Get a $100 Starbucks Gift Card](#)

Here Is a Handy Tabular Conversion Chart

	Tea spoon	Table spoon	fluid ounce	cup	pint	quart
1 tea spoon	1	1/3	1/6	----		
1 tablespoon	3	1	½	1/16	----	
1 fluid ounce	6	2	1	1/8	1/16	----
1 cup	48	16	8	1	½	¼
1 pint	96	32	16	2	1	½
1 quart	192	64	32	4	2	1

Get a $100 Starbucks Gift Card

1 teaspoon = 1/3 tablespoon = 1/6 fluid ounce

1 tablespoon = 3 teaspoons = ½ fluid oz. = 1/16 cup

1 fluid ounce = 6 tsp = 2 tbs = 1/8 cup = 1/16 pint

1 cup = 48 tsp. = 16 tbs. = 8 fluid oz. = ½ pint = ¼ quart

1 pint = 16 fluid oz. = 2 cups = ½ quart.

1 quart = 32 fluid oz. = 4 cups = 2 pints

1 bottle is 750ml

Get a $100 Starbucks Gift Card

Caramelized Espresso Frappe

Ingredients

¼ cup of hot cocoa mix
One cup of skim milk
¼ cup of sugar
¼ cup of water
½ cup of boiling water
2 teaspoons of instant coffee granules
1 cup of Crushed ice

Directions:

[1] dissolve the instant coffee granules in the hot water

[2] pour it into ice cube tray and refrigerate for several hours until it's solid

[3] in a small pot, dissolve the sugar in two tablespoons of water and apply medium heat until sugar dissolves and appears to be golden-brown (caramel)

[4] remove the pot from the heat source and add another 2 teaspoons of water to it. Stir

[5] whisk the caramel sugar and allow to cool

[6] pour the cocoa mix, milk and caramel sugar into a blender and blend the mixture until it is well blended

[7] while the blender is still running, bring out the frozen coffee ice cubes from the refrigerator and add them, one at a time, to the contents of the blender

[8] blend the mixture until it is smooth in appearance

[9] next, add crushed ice to the blender and blend further until it is smooth

[10] serve

Get a $100 Starbucks Gift Card

Caramel Apple Cider

Ingredients

1 cup of apple juice
1 teaspoon of caramel topping
1 teaspoon of whipped cream
1 teaspoon of cinnamon syrup

Directions:

[1] combine the cinnamon syrup and apple juice together in a saucepan and stir

[2] apply heat to the saucepan until the mixture is very hot

[3] pour out into suitable mugs and garnish with whipped cream

[4] top it up with caramel topping

[5] serve

Get a $100 Starbucks Gift Card

Caramel Macchiato

Ingredients

Caramel sauce
2 tablespoons of Vanilla syrup
Steamed milk
1 ½ cups of freshly brewed espresso

Directions:

[1] pour the vanilla syrup and the steamed milk together in a suitable coffee mug and stir

[2] add milk foam to the top of the mixture
[3] pour in freshly brewed espresso into the mug through the milk foam

[4] top up the drink with caramel sauce

[5] serve

Get a $100 Starbucks Gift Card

Cappuccino-Chocolate Coffee Cake

Ingredients

1/4 cup of sugar
1 egg
1/3 cup semisweet chocolate chips, melted
1/3 cup flaked coconut
1/4 cup of chopped nuts
1 tablespoon butter or margarine (melted)
2 cups Original Bisquick®
2/3 cup milk or water
1/4 cup sugar
2 tablespoons butter or margarine, melted
2 teaspoons powdered instant coffee (dry)

Directions

[1] pre-heat your oven to a temperature of about 400°F

[2] grease a medim sized square pan. Combine all the coconut, nuts, 1/4 cup of sugar and 1 tablespoon of butter and set them aside

[3] with the exception of the chocolate chips and coffee, place the remaining ingredients in bowl and beat them at low speed for about 30 seconds (ensure that you scrape bowl constantlywhile doing this)

[4] next, beat at medium speed for about 4 minutes while scraping the bowl occasionally. Pour out into the greased pan

[5] stir together the chocolate as well as the coffee; spoon over batter. Lightly swirl chocolate mixture through the batter several times with knife for marbled design

[6] sprinkle the coconut mixture evenly over the top.

[7] place this in your oven and bake for about 20 to 25 minutes or until it turns light golden brown

[8] Serve warm

Chai Tea

<u>Ingredients</u>

1 tsp ground cinnamon
½ tsp ground nutmeg
½ tsp ground cloves (use less than that if you don't like strong taste of clove)
3 cups water
3 cups milk (preferably skim milk)
½ cup of honey
1 tsp ground cardamom
½ tsp ground ginger (or a mashed small chunk of fresh)
6-8 black or decaf black tea bags

Directions

[1] mix the water and milk together in a saucer

[2] place the saucer on a heat source and bring to boil

[3] remove the saucer from the heat source and add all the other ingredients

[4] return the saucer to the heat source and bring to boil again

[5] once it has boiled, turn off the heat source and let steep for 3-5 minutes

[6] remove the tea bags then filter through a fine strainer

[7[serve hot or cold as desired

Get a $100 Starbucks Gift Card

Chocolate Cappuccino Mousse

Ingredients

1 teaspoon of vanilla extract
1½ cups of whipping cream
½ pound of bittersweet chocolate
1/4 cup of coffee syrup

Directions

[1] melt all of the chocolate and coffee syrup togetherin a double boiler over medium heat

[2] mix the cream and vanilla together in a bowl an whip them until soft peaks form. Slowly fold 1/4 of the whipped cream into the melted chocolate and after it has become well-blended, fold the remaining whipped cream into the chocolate

[3] spoon the mousse into dessert glasses and refrigertate

[4] If so desired, garnish the mousse with extra whipped cream and chocolate shavings

[5] serve

Coffee Italian Ices

Ingredients

½ cup of boiling water
1 cup of cold water
1/4 cup of sugar
2 tablespoons of instant espresso coffee powder
5 strawberries (if desired)

Directions

[1] mix the sugar and coffee powder together in a small bowl

[2] pour in the boiling water and stir until the mixture is completely dissolved

[3] add the cold water while stirring

[4] pour out the mixture into a 9x5x3-inch loaf pan or any suitable bowl and place in the freezer for about 2-3 hours or until it is firm

[5] break up the frozen mixture into smaller chunks with any suitable object and pour them into a chilled medium-sized bowl

[6] beat the chunks with an electric mixer on low speed until fluffy. Next, return this mixture to the freezer for another 2-3 hours or until firm

[7] whenever you're ready to serve, scoop the ice into small dessert dishes.

[8] If desired, garnish each serving with a strawberry

Coffee Banana Smoothie

Ingredients

Dash of ground nutmeg
¼ teaspoon of ground cinnamon
1 cup of skim milk
Fresh mint
8 ounces of coffee yoghurt
2 sliced frozen bananas

Directions:

[1] combine the milk, yogurt, frozen bananas, cinnamon and nutmeg together in a blender

[2] blend the ingredients until they appear to be smooth

[3] pour out the contents of the blender into suitable coffee mugs

[4] top up the coffee with fresh mint

[5] serve

Get a $100 Starbucks Gift Card

Double Chocolate Chip Crème Frappuchino

Ingredients

Crushed ice
4 tablespoons of chocolate chips
4 tablespoons of chocolate syrup
Whipped cream
4 cups of double-strength espresso

Directions:

[1]pour enough ice cubes in your blender to fill up to half its capacity

[2]next, add the espresso, chocolate syrup and chips to the contents of the blender

[3]blend the ingredients until it appears thick and smooth

[4]pour out into large mugs and top up with some whipped cream

[5]serve

Get a $100 Starbucks Gift Card

Eggnog Latte

Ingredients

Nutmeg
½ cup of eggnog
Starbucks espresso roast coffee (preferably ground)
¼ cup of whole milk or low-fat milk

Directions:

[1] in a clean container, mix the eggnog and the whole /low-fat milk together

[2] place this mixture in your espresso machine and set it to steam. When the temperature reaches about 150F, remove from the espresso machine

[3] pour in the ground espresso roast coffee into the coffee filter

[4] pour out desired quantity of espresso into your coffee mug and stir in some of the steamed milk and eggnog mix

[5] garnish with some nutmeg

[6] serve

Frozen Cappuccino

Ingredients

1/3 cup of ground Starbucks espresso roast coffee
1 cup of hot water
¾ cup of vanilla frozen yoghurt
2 tablespoons of sugar
½ cup of ice cubes

Directions:

[1]place the espresso coffee in a coffee filter and filter off the coffee using the hot water

[2]collect the filtered coffee in a suitable coffee mug and allow it to cool down

[3]next, pour the filtered coffee, vanilla frozen yoghurt, sugar and ice cubes into a blender and blend the ingredients until it becomes thick and smooth

[4]pour out the cappuccino into glass cups

{5}serve

Get a $100 Starbucks Gift Card

Frozen Cappuccino #2

Ingredients

2 teaspoons of coffee syrup
2 teaspoons of sugar
1/8 teaspoon of ground cinnamon
¼ cup of evaporated skim milk
1/3 cup of freshly brewed coffee

Directions:

[1]pour all of the freshly brewed coffee into ice cube trays and refrigerate for several hours until they become frozen

[2]once the coffee becomes frozen into cubes, remove from the refrigerator and pour them into a blender

[3]add the sugar, ground cinnamon, skim milk and coffee syrup to the blender and blend the ingredients into a fine puree

[4]serve

Frozzen Caramel Frappucino

Ingredients

1 cup of low-fat milk
2 cups of ice
¾ cup of cold double-strength coffee
3 tablespoons of granulated sugar
3 tablespoons of caramel topping
Whipped cream

Directions

[1] prepare the double strength coffee by using twice the regular quantity required by your favorite coffee maker or 2 tsps of groung coffee for each cup of coffee

[2] pour the first 4 ingrdients listed above into a blender and blend together at high speed till the mixture comes out smooth and all the ice has become crushed

[3] serve in ice glasses

[4] top each glass with whipped cream

[5] drizzle additional caramel over the whipped cream

Frozzen Mocha Frappucino

Ingredients

3 tablespoons Hershey's chocolate syrup
1 cup of low-fat milk
2 cups of ice
¾ cup of cold double-strength coffee
3 tablespoons of granulated sugar
Whipped cream

Directions

[1] prepare the double strength coffee by using twice the regular quantity required by your favorite coffee maker or 2 tsps of groung coffee for each cup of coffee

[2] pour the first 5 ingredients listed above into a blender and blend together at high speed till the mixture comes out smooth and all the ice has become crushed

[3] serve in ice glasses

[4] top each glass with whipped cream if desired

Frozzen Frappucino

Ingredients

1 cup of low-fat milk
2 cups of ice
¾ cup of cold double-strength coffee
3 tablespoons of granulated sugar

Directions

[1] prepare the double strength coffee by using twice the regular quantity required by your favorite coffee maker or 2 tsps of groung coffee for each cup of coffee

[2] pour all the above ingrdients into a blender and blend together at high speed till the mixture comes out smooth and all the ice has become crushed

[3] serve in ice glasses

Gingerbread Latte

Ingredients

Ground nutmeg
3 tablespoons of starbucks gingerbread syrup
3 cups of steamed milk
2 shots of starbucks espresso pods

Directions:

[1] pour the gingerbread syrup into a warm coffee mug

[2] brew the shots of espresso coffee and pour the coffee into the coffee mug containing the gingerbread syrup

[3] add the steamed milk and its foam to the coffee

[4] for garnishing, add a dash of nutmeg to the coffee

[5] serve

Get a $100 Starbucks Gift Card

Harvest Coffee Cider

Ingredients

3 cups of cold water
1 cup of apple juice
¼ cup of brown sugar
¼ teaspoon of ground cinnamon
1/4 cup of ground Maxwell House coffee

Directions:

[1] pour the ground coffee in the brew basket of your preferred coffee maker

[2] add cinnamon to the ground coffee in the coffee maker

[3] pour the apple juice and sugar in the coffee maker's pot.

[4] add the 3 cups of water to the coffee maker and then proceed to brew

[5] stir the coffee and serve

Get a $100 Starbucks Gift Card

Hot Mocha

Ingredients

3 cups of skim milk
½ teaspoon of vanilla
2 tablespoons of cocoa powder
2 tablespoons of sugar
2 teaspoons of instant coffee

Directions:

[1] get a small pot and mix the cocoa powder, sugar and instant coffee together

[2] next, slowly stir in the skim milk into the mixture until the mixture becomes very smooth

[3] place the pot on heat source and apply medium heat until the mixture becomes very hot

[4] remove the pot from the heat source and add the vanilla to it. Stir

[5] pour out into mugs and serve

Get a $100 Starbucks Gift Card

Iced Constantine Coffee

Ingredients

Ice cubes
Half and half milk
2/3 cup of honey
½ teaspoon of ground cardamom
6 cups of water
2/3 cup of dark roast coffee
4 diced cinnamon sticks

Directions:

[1]mix the 6 cups of water with the cinnamon sticks and roast coffee

[2]brew the mixture and add the cardamom and honey to the prepared coffee.

[3]stir to dissolve the honey and allow to cool. Place in the refrigerator to chill

[4]when you're ready to serve, put some ice cubes in your coffee mug and pour out the coffee into it

[5] stir in some half and half milk

[6]serve

Iced Espresso

Ingredients

Ice cubes
4 cups of water
1 cup of skim milk
1 teaspoon of grated orange peel
½ cup of ground espresso coffee
3 tablespoons of sugar
1 teaspoon of grated chocolate shavings/chips

Directions:

[1]mix both the ground espresso coffee and grated orange peel in your coffee maker and brew them together

[2]pour out the brewed coffee into a suitable container and add sugar and milk to it

[3] place in the refrigerator to chill

[4]whenever you're ready to serve the coffee, put ice cubes in your coffee mug and pour in the coffee. Stir

[5]garnish with grated chocolate shavings

[6]serve

Iced Caramel Macchiato

Ingredients

Ice cubes
Whipped cream
Caramel sauce
2 tablespoons of Vanilla syrup
Cold milk
1 ½ cups of freshly brewed espresso

Directions:

[1]pour out the vanilla syrup into a mug. Add milk to the mug (fill up to about half the volume of the mug)

[2]pour some ice cubes in the mug followed by the espresso

[3]garnish with some whipped cream and top up with the caramel sauce

[4]serve

Get a $100 Starbucks Gift Card

Irish cream espresso

Ingredients

2 large eggs
1 large egg white
½ cup of sugar
3 tablespoons of Irish cream (such as Bailey's)
1 tablespoon of instant espresso (2 tablespoons instant coffee granules)
1/3 cup of sugar
3 tablespoons of water
cooking spray
1/8 teaspoon of salt
1 (12-ounce) can evaporated skim milk
Chopped chocolate-covered coffee beans (optional)

Directions

[1] pre-heat your oven to a temperature of about 325 F

[2] in a medium sized pan, dissolve the 1/3 cup of sugar in the 3 tablespoons of water and place the pan over medium-high heat

[3] heat the mixture for about 5-8 minutes until all the sugar dissolves and turns golden in colur (while stirring frequently)

[4] coat the interiors of 4 custard cups (or any other suitable containers) with cooking spray and pour the sugar mixture into them while tilting each cup quickly as you pour until caramelized sugar coats bottom of cup. Set aside.

[5] whisk the eggs and egg white in a medium bowl and stir in the ½ cup of sugar, liqueur, espresso, salt, and milk

[6] share this prepared mixture evenly among the custard cups. Next, place cups in a 9-inch square baking pan and add hot water to pan to a depth of 1 inch

[7] place this in your oven and bake at 325° for a 45 - 50 minutes or until when a knife inserted into the center comes out clean. When you bake to this stage, remove the cups from pan

[8] cover and refrigerate for at least 4 hours

[9] next, remove from the custard cups by loosen edges of custards with a knife or rubber spatula

[10] place a dessert plate, upside down, on top of each cup and invert them onto plates

[11] if you have any remaining caramelized syrup, you can pour them over the custards with a spoon

[12] garnish with the chopped coffee beans, if desired

[13] serve

Get a $100 Starbucks Gift Card

Java Float

Ingredients

1 cups of chilled club soda
2 scoops of coffee ice cream
2 tablespoons of chocolate syrup

Directions:

[1]in a tall glass cup, pour two tablespoons of chocolate syrup and stir in the cup of chilled club soda

[2]next, add the two scoops of coffee ice cream to the glass

[3]serve

Get a $100 Starbucks Gift Card

Minty Hot Mocha

Ingredients

½ teaspoon of peppermint extracts
2 tablespoons of instant coffee
1 cup of water
¼ cup of sugar
¼ cup of unsweetened cocoa
4 ½ cups of skim milk

Directions:

[1]mix both the sugar and unsweetened cocoa together in a saucer

[2]add water to the mixture and stir

[3]place the saucer on a heat source. While stirring continuously, apply medium heat till it boils

[4]add the coffee to the solution followed by the milk (add milk in small portions)

[5]heat the mixture while stirring it until it becomes very hot

[6]remove the saucer from the heat source and add the peppermint extracts

[7]whisk the solution until it become frothy

[8]serve

Mocha Java

Ingredients

1 tablespoon of sugar
1 cup of strong fresh coffee
2 tablespoons of semi-sweet chocolate
¼ cup of half-and-half

Directions:

[1] pour the coffee, sugar and semi-sweet chocolate into a saucer

[2] place the saucer on a heat source and heat the ingredients until all of the sugar has dissolved and the chocolate has melted

[3] pour out the half and half milk into a separate small pot and warm it until it becomes very warm/steaming

[4] pour the contents of the saucer into a suitable coffee mug

[5] pour in the hot half and half into the coffee mug and stir

[6] serve

Mocha Mudslide

Ingredients

2 tablespoons of sugar
1 teaspoon of instant coffee
¼ cup of vanilla low-fat yoghurt
1 cup of fat-free milk
2/3 cup of sliced bananas

Directions:

[1]place the instant coffee, sugar, milk and sliced bananas together in a blender

[2]blend the ingredients together until the mixture is smooth

[3]pour out the contents of the blender into a clean container and refrigerate it until the mixture becomes a little bit solidified

[4]return this solidified mixture to the blender and add the yoghurt

[5]blend for a few minutes until the resulting mixture appears smooth in appearance

[6]serve

Mocha Coconut Frappuccino

Ingredients

1 cup of low-fat milk
Whipped cream
2 cups of ice
¾ cup of double strength coffee
½ cup of shredded coconut
3 tablespoons of sugar
1/3 cup of Hershey's chocolate syrup

Directions:

[1] first, the shredded coconut must be toasted in the oven. The oven should be pre-heated to a temperature of about 320 degrees

[2] wrap the coconut in aluminum foil and place in the oven. the shredded coconut should be toasted for about half an hour and turned frequently while being toasted

[3] once that is done, combine only 1/3rd of the toasted coconut (leave some for later), the double-strength coffee, milk, chocolate syrup and sugar together in a blender

[4] blend these ingredients for a few seconds

[5]add the ice cubes into the blender and blend further till the mixture becomes smooth

[6]pour out the drink into tall glass cups and garnish with whipped cream

[7]top up the drink with some of the leftover toasted coconut and chocolate syrup

[8]serve

Get a $100 Starbucks Gift Card

Mocha Slush

Ingredients

2 cups of non-fat milk
6 cups of freshly-brewed double-strength coffee
2/3 cup of unsweetened cocoa powder

Directions:

[1] pour 3 cups out of the double-strength coffee into ice cube trays and refrigerate until they are frozen

[2] in a clean container, pour the remaining 3 cups of double-strength coffee and stir in the milk and cocoa powder

[3] remove the frozen coffee cubes from the refrigerator once they are frozen and crush them with a hammer or any hard object

[4] pour the crushed iced coffee cubes into coffee mugs

[5] add the coffee mixture in the container to the coffee mug

[6] top up the drink with some cocoa powder

[7] serve

Peppermint Mocha

Ingredients

¼ cup of double-strength, dark roasted coffee
3 tablespoons of starbucks mocha powder
Whipped cream
12 ounces of steamed milk
2 tablespoons of starbucks peppermint syrup
Red sugar sprinkles

Directions:

[1] mix the 3 tablespoons of starbucks mocha powder with 3 tablespoons of hot water and stir thoroughly to make a syrup

[2] pour this syrup into a suitable coffee mug and add to it the roasted coffee

[3] next, add the peppermint syrup to the mix

[4] stir in the steamed milk and stir

[5] garnish with whipped cream and the red sugar sprinkles

[6] serve

Pumpkin Spice Latte

Ingredients

1 tablespoon of white mocha Tollhouse chips
2 tablespoons of pumpkin spice
2 shots of espresso
3 ounces of milk
3 ounces of half and half
 Whipped cream

Directions:

[1]mix the half and half and the milk together in a saucepan and steam the mixture

[2]pour into a tall glass cup and add the espresso and chips. Stir

[3]garnish it with whipped cream and some of the pumpkin spice

[4]serve

Simple One Cup Chai

Ingredients

¾ inch piece of ginger (crushed)
2 tbsps of Darjeeling tea leaves
2 tbsps of sugar
2 cups of milk
2 cups of water

Directions

[1] bring the water to boil

[2] add the crushed ginger to the water and leave to boil for few more minutes

[3] pour the tea leaves and leave to steep for 2 – 3 minutes

[4] strain the tea and add milk and sugar as desired

[5] serve

Starbucks Chai Tea

Ingredients

2 tablespoons of ground cardamom
2 tablespoons of ground cinnamon
½ a cup of honey
3 cups of milk
3 cups of water
8 black tea bags
½ teaspoon of nutmeg
½ teaspoon of ground cloves
½ teaspoon of ground ginger

Directions:

[1] pour the milk and water into a saucepan

[2] place the saucepan on a heat source and bring to boil with medium heat

[3] when the mixture has boiled, remove from the heat source and add all of the other ingredients

[4] return the saucepan to the heat source and bring to boil again

[5] when it has boiled, remove from the heat and allow it to steep for about 5 minutes

[6] discard the tea bags and filter off any residue or particles using a strainer or sieve

[7] serve hot or cold as desired

Starbucks Frappuccino

Ingredients

¼ cup of sugar
½ cup of freshly brewed espresso
1 tablespoon of dry pectin
2 ½ cups of low fat milk

Directions:

[1]in a suitable mug or container, pour the espresso and low-fat milk together

[2]add the sugar and dry pectin. Stir until the sugar dissolves completely

[3]place in the refrigerator to chill

[4]serve while it's cold

Get a $100 Starbucks Gift Card

Starbucks Frozen Frappuccino

Ingredients

1 cup of low-fat milk
2 cups of ice
3 tablespoons of sugar
¾ cup of freshly brewed double-strength espresso

Directions:

[1] after brewing the double-strength coffee, place it in the refrigerator to chill before proceeding

[2] when the coffee is cold, pour into the blender with the milk, sugar and ice cubes

[3] blend the ingredients until the mixture become smooth in appearance

[4] pour out the drink in tall glass cups and serve

Get a $100 Starbucks Gift Card

Starbucks Vanilla Iced Coffee

Ingredients

Milk
1 ½ tablespoons of Fontana vanilla syrup
Ice cubes
8 ounces of freshly-brewed double-strength coffee

Directions:

[1]once the double-strength coffee has been brewed, place in the refrigerator to chill

[2]once chilled, pour the cold coffee over ice cubes in a suitable mug

[3]stir in the vanilla syrup and milk

[4]serve

Starbucks White Chocolate Mocha

Ingredients

Whipped cream
2/3 cup of whole milk
6 tablespoons of white chocolate chips
2 cups of freshly brewed coffee

Directions:

[1] pour the milk and the chocolate chips together in saucer

[2] apply medium heat to the saucer while stirring frequently. Heat till the chips melt

[3] get a clean coffee pitcher or container and pour in the milk mixture from the saucer. Add the freshly brewed coffee and stir

[4] garnish with whipped cream and serve

Get a $100 Starbucks Gift Card

Starbucks Spiced Holiday Coffee

Ingredients

6 cups of water
2/3 cup of honey
½ teaspoon of ground cardamom
4 crushed sticks of cinnamon
2/3 cup of ground Starbucks Christmas Blend
milk

Directions:

[1]pour the crushed cinnamon sticks, coffee and water together into your coffee maker and brew the coffee

[2]add the ground cardamom and honey to the brewed coffee. Stir to dissolve the honey

[3pour in the coffee to fill about 2/3rd of the volume of the coffee mug. Make up the rest of the volume with the milk

[4]serve

Get a $100 Starbucks Gift Card

Table of Contents

Caramelized Espresso Frappe
Caramel Apple Cider
Caramel Macchiato
Cappuccino-Chocolate Coffee Cake
Chai Tea
Chocolate Cappuccino Mousse
Coffee Banana Smoothie
Coffee Italian Ices
Double Chocolate Chip Crème Frappuccino
Eggnog Latte
Frozen Cappuccino
Frozen Cappuccino #2
Frozzen Caramel Frappucino
Frozzen Frappucino
Frozzen Mocha Frappucino
Gingerbread Latte
Harvest Coffee Cider
Hot Mocha
Iced Constantine Coffee
Iced Espresso
Iced Caramel Macchiato

Irish cream espresso
Java Float
Minty Hot Mocha
Mocha Java
Mocha Mudslide
Mocha Coconut Frappuccino
Mocha Slush
Peppermint Mocha
Pumpkin Spice Latte
Simple One Cup Chai
Starbucks Chai Tea
Starbucks Frappuccino
Starbucks Frozen Frappuccino
Starbucks Vanilla Iced Coffee
Starbucks White Chocolate Mocha
Starbucks Spiced Holiday Coffee

About the Author

Jennifer James is a single mother of four children. She lives in Chicago and spends much of her time reading, writing and cooking which are her greatest passions.

In her spare time, she enjoys swimming, spending time with her children and pet dogs.

She has also worked in corporate public relations.

For more books by Jennifer James, CLICK HERE to visit her official page.

Get a $100 Starbucks Gift Card

CPSIA information can be obtained
at www.ICGtesting.com
Printed in the USA
LVHW081315100321
681095LV00014B/263